An Edwardian Family Album

An Edwardian Family Album

Lesley Richmond

LOCHAR PUBLISHING
MOFFAT
SCOTLAND

In memory of my father who
might have read this one

© Lesley Richmond & University of Glasgow Archives,
1991

Published by Lochar Publishing Ltd
MOFFAT DG10 9ED

British Library Cataloguing in Publication Data
Richmond, Lesley **1956**–
    An Edwardian Family Album
    I. Title
    779.99411

ISBN 0-948403-65-9

Book Design by Mark Blackadder.

Typeset in 11 on 13pt Goudy Old Style by
Chapterhouse, Formby.
Printed by Eagle Colourbooks Ltd, Scotland

Contents

Acknowledgements

All these photographs are reproduced by kind permission of the University of Glasgow. William Lind of Bridge of Weir is owed a great deal of thanks for discovering the collection, purchasing it and subsequently donating it to the Archives Department of the University.

I should like to thank the following people for their help in compiling this book: Duncan Cameron of Corstorphine, a member of the Cameron family who can remember visiting and going on outings with 'Uncle William', for providing most useful details about the Jackson Family not least the Lattimer link; Michael Moss, Archivist for the University of Glasgow for his most useful comments on the text and photographs; Arnott Wilson, Archivist for the City of Edinburgh District Council, for providing details about the Edinburgh homes and grave of W F Jackson; Iain Russell of the University of Glasgow, for his most valuable research work; and David Richmond for all his support and forbearance with yet another project.

Introcduction

The Edwardian Era

When the fifty-nine year-old Edward Saxe-Coburg succeeded to the throne in 1901 the British people eagerly anticipated the change a new monarch would bring to the country and their lives. Within twenty years the Great War had affected and changed everyone's life in ways no-one could have anticipated. Although Edward died in 1910, the Edwardian Era, the period of history named after him, continued until the outbreak of the war.

The first fourteen years of the twentieth century, following on from the restrictive Victorian age, were to take on the mantle of a halcyon age for at least the upper and middle classes of Scotland. Even to the lowest class of people in Scotland, the reality of the hardships of the Edwardian years was transformed into a memory of golden days before the carnage of the war in which 110,000 lives were lost, equivalent to about ten per cent of the Scottish male population aged between sixteen and fifty years of age. For those who survived the First World War, the Edwardian Age was remembered as being ordered, prosperous and sunny. Although of just fourteen years duration, it left a deep impression on British history and culture, in dress, art, music, drama, morals, and the image of affluence. The lasting picture image is one of 'upstairs, downstairs'.

The Edwardian era was one of great extremes of riches and penury, inequalities caused by the accident of birth. There were four main social classes: the upper, containing the old landed gentry and the *nouveau riche* who had made their money as a result of the Industrial Revolution of the previous century; the middle, split into upper and lower sections to differentiate between the professionals and small businessmen; the working, by far the largest proportion, both rural and urban, skilled and unskilled, again split into different status groups; and the unemployed poor of the city clums and the rural countryside. Social status was defined in all households by the number of servants. Even the households of the lower classes had a live-in or daily help. There were more workers in domestic service than any other occupation during the Edwardian era. Wages were low, the hours long and time-off a luxury, but domestic service was an honourable occupation for a working class girl.

The middle classes had a way of life mirrored on that of the upper classes, servants, the social round of calls, tea parties, dinner

The leisure class of 1909. Mrs Jackson entertaining a few of
her friends in the garden at the back of 'Glenlyon', the
holiday house that the Jacksons rented in Gullane, East
Lothian, for the summers of 1909 to 1911. Umbrellas are
being used as makeshift parasols to keep off the worst of the
sun's rays. The doll being held by one of the women must
have belonged to one of the girls sitting on the rug,
engrossed with Snark the dog and avoiding the eye of the
camera.

parties, visits to the theatre, seaside holidays at home and tours abroad. The lower working classes lived in badly ventilated and badly heated housing with little sanitation and worked for long hours for little reward for most of their lives. It was indeed an age of extremes in wealth and poverty.

William Fulton Jackson

William Fulton Jackson, the son of John Jackson, was born in Glasgow in 1855 and was educated at St Enoch's Parish School, being awarded its Dux Medal in his sixteenth year. He worked as a junior clerk in the offices of Messrs Westlands, Laidlaw & Co, hatters, of Howard Street, Glasgow, for five years prior to his promotion to the position of cashier and book keeper. In February 1877 he took up a post in the office of the Secretary of the North British Railway Company, one of the leading railway companies in Scotland, and was soon given the direction of the Rates and Taxes Department. In this position he succeeded in effecting various important savings, a success which brought him the favourable notice of the directors of the company. He was selected in 1898 by the five Scottish Railway Companies, the Caledonian, Glasgow and South-Western, Great North of Scotland, Highland and North British, to give evidence on their behalf before the Royal Commission on Local Taxation. In June 1899 he was appointed general manager of the North British Railway Company. He held the post until his retirement, chiefly for reasons of health, in the spring of 1918. As general manager of the North British he was involved with many railway company mergers and saw the company's profits rise substantially. It was said of W F Jackson that he had walked over every portion of the 1,250 miles of the North British line.

The North British Railway Company was associated with Edinburgh, in the same way that the Caledonian Railway Company was regarded as the Glasgow system. Its branches, however, extended to Mallaig, Inverness-shire, in the north-west, Silloth, Cumbria, in the south-west, Aberdeen in the north-east, and Newcastle-upon-Tyne in the south-east. In 1901 it had an annual train mileage of 18,000,000 miles and an annual passenger traffic – exclusive of season ticket holders – of 38,000,000 persons, an annual goods and mineral traffic of over 22,000,000 tons, a capital of nearly £59 million and an annual income of nearly £4.5 million. At the February annual general meeting of the company in 1918, at which he retired, W F Jackson received many tributes to his services from the chairman of the North British and others. It was said in his obituary in the *Scotsman*, 2 December 1931, that he:

> ...*was always kindly and considerate. He had an old world courtesy and the unwavering devotion from which he served the company was freely acknowledged by all associated with him in its management.*

Mr and Mrs W F Jackson in the garden of their holiday house, 'Bellemore' in September 1910. The patchy untidy grass is a sure sign that it was cut by hand and not by machine. The owner of the garden was a keen horticulturalist as the chrysanthemums and the elaborate frame supporting the sweet peas testify.

Miss Janet (Jenny) Cameron carrying one of the two cameras used by W F Jackson in his photography. It is a folding roll-film camera which had the viewfinder at waist height, explaining the low viewpoint of the photographs in this book. Miss Cameron and Mrs Jackson are standing on a rustic bridge at the Black Rock of Novar, Evanton, near Dingwall, Cromarty in September 1912.

The head offices of the North British Railway Company at
No. 23 Waterloo Place, Edinburgh. The flowers in the
window boxes look resplendent in the August sunshine.
The grand ornate lamp posts stand outside No. 25 the
offices of the Edinburgh and Leith Gas Commissioners.

John Thomas, the author of the definitive history of the North British Railway Company, having studied the surviving records of the company formed a different opinion about him. He writes:

The cosy obituaries of W F Jackson, North British general manager, in the contemporary railway press contain no hint of the tyrant revealed by his letters in the North British Company's letter books.

He adds, he was 'a good railwayman but a firebrand of the first order', fastidious about spitting on trains and vandalism on special workers' services. Certainly one of his great-nephews recalls that, even towards the end of his life, the news that W F Jackson was on his way in the first class compartment of the next train ensured that the station master was ready and waiting on the platform to meet the man when the train pulled into the station.

W F Jackson married Margaret McJennart Lattimer, who had two sisters, Marion and Elizabeth, and a brother, John. Marion married Duncan Cameron and Elizabeth married Robert Readdie and thus established the link among many of the families in the photograph albums. W F Jackson was a prominent layman, in turn, of the Free Church, United Free Church and Church of Scotland, as the Scottish presbyterian churches merged in the early twentieth century, in both Glasgow and Edinburgh. He was always an active church worker, especially with young people. From his early twenties he was an enthus-

iastic member of the Young Men's Christian Association, joining the George Square Branch of the Glasgow Young Men's Society for Religious Improvement in 1874. He served on its Evangelistic Committee for many years and led the early Sabbath bible study and fellowship meetings. After he joined the North British Railway Company and moved to Edinburgh, he continued for a considerable time to travel back to Glasgow at weekends to carry on this work. Within the congregations in which he was a member in Edinburgh he was an enthusiastic supporter of the Band of Hope and Literary Societies. He initially lived in the Murrayfield area of west Edinburgh and served as an elder at Roseburn Free Church. Following his appointment as general manager of the North British he moved to 29 Royal Terrace and subsequently to 12 Carlton Terrace. While he lived on Calton Hill he was an active member and elder of the Guthrie Memorial United Free Church in Easter Road. By May 1916 he had moved into a much larger property, Suffolk House, 18 Suffolk Road, Newington, where he became an elder of Mayfield United Free Church.

W F Jackson was widely read and had a special interest in science and astrology, lecturing on these subjects and mineralogy. He collected many items of interest and specimens of natural history from his travels to the Continent and Northern Europe, his house in Suffolk Road containing a private museum of his curios, fondly remembered by many of his young relatives. His collection of 'rocks' was donated to the Geology Department of Glasgow University in the late 1950s. He was a successful general manager of the North British Railway Company but, if it had not been for his skill as a photographer, he would have been lost in the footnotes of railway history. The photographs he took of his family provide a close up view of the life of the middle classes in the Edwardian Era, while his views of other people and places, often at a greater distance from the camera, reveal more of society at large prior to the First World War.

The Photographs

All the photographs in this book are to be found in the Jackson Collection in the Archives of the University of Glasgow. William Lind of Bridge of Weir discovered this collection of family photo-graph albums in a Glasgow saleroom in the late 1970s. He immediately recognised their historical worth and purchased the collection, subse-quently donating them to the Archives Depart-ment of the University. The identity of the photographer, however, remained a mystery until George Oliver, a professional photographer and freelance writer, featured the photographs in two consecutive issues of *The Scots Magazine* in the winter of 1980, in which he descibed them as having been:

> . . . assembled . . . by an unknown Edinburgh photographer – evidently a comfortably-off and widely travelled amateur with far above average

W F Jackson did not take all the photographs which appear in the albums. The second photographer was usually Jenny Cameron. Her brother James is holding the other camera which is a smaller version of the one in another photograph. His sister Marion and Mr and Mrs Jackson have posed for this picture whilst out walking on the beach at North Berwick, East Lothian in September 1910.

Mrs George Carse, Mrs W F Jackson and Marion Cameron inspecting some of W F Jackson's photographic work in the garden at 'Faussethill', Gullane. More albums are yet to be inspected but no one looks impressed. These are the albums that form part of the Jackson Collection in the Archives of Glasgow University.

pictorial appreciation. There is abundant evidence of high technical proficiency which enabled him, or her, to overcome the limitations of contemporary films and equipment.

The photographs were recognised by readers, descendants of W F Jackson's relatives, the subject of so many of the photographs and so the identity of the principal photographer was revealed.

The collection of photographs which now bear his name consist of 128 albums containing over 14,500 contact prints of people and places throughout Great Britain, Continental and Northern Europe and Egypt between the years 1902 and 1938, the vast majority being taken between 1904 and 1918. There are also over 14,500 original negatives on plastic and both prints and negatives are in very good condition. They were taken with box or folding roll-film cameras of two different sizes, held, usually, at chest or waist height. For technical reasons (large format cameras, slow film and lens type) it was difficult to obtain good quality interior photographs but W F Jackson sometimes took his camera indoors and occasionally achieved a high quality shot. The collection is also unusual in that the photographs are nearly all precisely dated with the day, month and year and they are all captioned, identifying the people and locations.

Since the collection of photographs has been in the Archives of Glasgow University it has been catalogued with the help of persons employed under the former Manpower Services Commission Scheme. The catalogue has been computerised so that it is possible to search for photographs by the name of the person photographed; the location, by both town and country; by its subject, as described by the caption, for example, fishing, ploughing, farms, churches; and by its date. The photographs themselves are of a high technical standard, to quote George Oliver:

When I opened one [album]...any doubts I might have had were quickly dispelled. Family albums these might be but the overall standard of photography was greatly above the average. These pictures were sharp, correctly exposed, often pictorially exciting because their maker broke the rules on occasion. There was nothing slapdash about the manner of their taking – the usual major fault of family photography – but a concern for proper placing of people and places, an awareness of the quality of light at different times of day and year...

William Fulton Jackson was a member of the middle class and so his collection of photographs, not surprisingly, portray the comfortable life of the Scottish middle classes in the Edwardian period. However, on the whole they do not give the appearance of being taken merely by a curious tourist but by a documentary photographer recording the world around him, his family, his travels and his work.

No. 12 Carlton Terrace, Edinburgh, the home of Mr and Mrs W F Jackson from 1903 to 1918. Note the Victorian hexagonal post box from which many of the family's postcards which feature in the Jackson collection must have been posted. Today a more modern postbox stands in its place. The gate on the right in the railings would have been the tradesmen's entrance leading down to the kitchen and servants's rooms. The Terrace was part of a development which lasted many years as the stonework joining No. 12 to its neighbour demonstrates. Setts were used as a road surface during this period and lasted well into the 1960s in many Scottish towns. These ones have not yet been removed.

Home Life

The homes of the Edwardian middle classes in Edinburgh have a solid and respectable air to the late twentieth-century eye. William Fulton Jackson's home at No. 12 Carlton Terrace stood at the junction of Carlton Terrace and Easter Road, to the east of Calton Hill, and it is no exception. Carlton Terrace, built in the 1820s, was situated on the apex of a curving triangle formed by Royal Terrace to the north and Regent Terrace to the south. No. 12 was a typical terraced house of the upper middle class and would have had the family living rooms and the formal reception rooms on the ground and first floors, the bedrooms and dressing rooms on the upper floors and the servants' rooms and living areas, the kitchen, pantries and wine cellar in the basement. There was no front garden and only a small walled garden to the back of the house but the occupants of the houses in Carlton Terrace had exclusive access to the Royal Terrace Gardens which ran in front of the Terrace where walks could be taken. The majority of houses during the period were still lighted by gas.

W F Jackson undoubtedly walked the three-quarters of a mile to his office in Waterloo Place from his home in Carlton Terrace. He moved to Suffolk House, 18 Suffolk Road, Newington, in 1916, and after his wife's death in October 1918 Miss Janet (Jenny to the family) Cameron, his niece, looked after him, acting as the mistress of the house. It would appear that Miss Cameron had been a permanent part of the Jackson household, sharing in holidays and other trips, for many years prior to that date. Mr and Mrs Jackson never had children of their own.

The Jacksons like all members of their class had servants, at least two were photographed by W F Jackson. Even in the households of the lower middle classes – the clerks, the lowlier civil servants, the shopkeepers and the teachers – there was nearly always a resident servant – a cook general, while in the more prosperous homes there would be a cook and various maids. In nearly every middle class home there was a piano around which the family and guests entertained themselves, or recited, sang or played some other instrument. Home life was single sexed during the week in middle class households where the women of the house entertained friends with the assistance of their female servants while the men where at the office. Whist and bridge were popular card games of the period. Meals were also important social occasions and in middle class homes food was plentiful at family meals and tea and dinner parties. During the summer *al fresco* entertaining was also very popular.

The drawing room at 12 Carlton Terrace in March 1913. The Jackson, Cameron and Readdie cousins sit around the ubiquitous piano while their elders inspect a photograph album. Interior photographs were very difficult for the photographer and tiring for the sitter and the ghost like figure is Miss Jeanie Cameron who moved during the long exposure time. There are many framed paintings and photographs on the walls and the mirrored dresser is overflowing with ornaments but the room on the whole feels uncluttered. Wall gas lights can be seen on both sides of the dresser.

An ornate china plant holder in the drawing room. The detail of the flowered wallpaper can be clearly seen. The room's overall appearance is one of lightness, the dark colours of the Victorian era have been replaced. Along with the Turner print hanging on the wall is a framed photograph of Mrs W F Jackson.

Lunch at 'Glenlyon', 12 June 1911. Mrs Jackson is ladling a
helping of soup from the tureen, perhaps it is for the
photographer whose place is empty. Miss Nellie Jackson
(W F Jackson's sister), Mrs John Jackson, Senior, Miss Janet
Cameron and Miss Mary Jackson have started their lunch.
The meal is to be washed down with water and the table is
dominated by a large jar of mixed pickles. Note the silver
tea pots and oil lamps on the sideboard – 'Glenlyon' was
not lit by gas – and the serviceable and durable linoleum on
the floor under the table.

Afternoon tea in the dining room at 'Glenlyon', 1909. Mrs
Jackson and her sister Elizabeth, Mrs Robert Readdie, are
about to partake of bread, sugared buns, tea cakes and
fancies. Four vases of roses set off the table laid with fine
china and starched napkins.

A sewing bee in the drawing room at 'Glenlyon'. Miss
Nellie Jackson and her sister-in-law, Mrs W F Jackson, are
sewing lace edging while her mother, Mrs John Jackson,
Senior, is crocheting. The tiled fireplace with a mirrored
overmantle is typical of the period. Flowers in vases and
adorning mirrors, pictures and the wallpaper decorate the
room.

'Faussethill', the Jackson's holiday home in Main Street,
Gullane for the summers of 1912 to 1914. It is Edwardian or
'turn of the century' in style with some mock Tudor
timbering and the property consisted of a detached house,
garden, stables and coach-house. The house was owned by
James Wood, a farmer in Gullane who rented it out to
summer visitors. 'Faussethill', with its stone eagle above the
entrance porch, was the grandest of all the houses the
Jacksons rented in Gullane.

Miss E McGhie (perched on a piano stool), Mrs W F
Jackson, Miss M F Readdie and Miss M McGhie playing
whist in the drawing room of 'Faussethill' on 17 August
1912. They are studying their cards very intently while
keeping their backs perfectly straight. A bowl of cherries
sits on the middle of the table. 'Faussethill' unlike
'Glenlyon' is lit by gas – a gas light
can be seen above the
picture.

Margaret Nicholson, one of the servants at 12 Carlton Terrace, Edinburgh, in 1904. Margaret's apron and cap are grander than those of Mary, in another photograph, so perhaps this is the above stairs maid. Mrs Jackson is knitting socks, they could be for her husband or one of her many male relatives. The narrowness of the town gardens to the back of the houses in Carlton Terrace can be clearly seen.

Mary MacLeod, another servant at 12 Carlton Terrace, Edinburgh, in 1909. Her white apron is well starched but she has torn the hem. Her collar and cuffs would have been very uncomfortable as they are made from hard celluloid. The ivy has grown sufficiently in five years to hide the ugly garden wall.

Miss Nellie McGill a servant at 'Glenlyon', Gullane, in July 1911. She may have been brought by the Jacksons from Edinburgh or have been hired locally for the summer. Her teeth demonstrate the horrors which resulted from the Scottish love of sugar and sweet food before the days of good denture provision.

Miss Jane Howden at 'Faussethill', Gullane, in May 1912. Her collar is not made of hard plastic but of material and she has a small neck bow. Her mop cap is also different from the other domestic servants pictured here so perhaps she was a local girl hired for the summer.

Jane at work serving tea in the garden at 'Faussethill' on 30 July 1912. Jenny Cameron has stopped playing golf to supervise the operations. The richly decorated tea cosy is probably keeping warm a silver tea pot, its matching sugar bowl can be clearly seen on the oblong table.

During the summer, afternoon tea in the garden was a very
popular occasion for entertaining family, friends and
acquaintances. On this warm, sunny day in late May 1912,
Jenny Cameron is offering the guests cakes and buns from a
cake stand covered in decorative doilies, while Mrs W F
Jackson is passing Miss Elma Carse a cup of tea. Two deck
chairs have been placed alongside the garden bench to
provide seating for the party while the tables have been
brought out from the house.

Queen Street, Glasgow, looking north towards Queen Street Station, of the North British Railway, 22 February 1913. The delivery and collecting boys are hard at work going about their various duties. The boy on the right is about to feed the horse, while the old woman and boy on the pavement on the left are collecting firewood. An apothecary's mortar and pestle shop-sign can be seen above the herbalist on the right and a large pair of spectacles denotes the opticians on the left.

Light traffic on a quiet Princes Street, Edinburgh, West End, March 1913. Pedestrians have no trouble in crossing the road. A variety of vehicles move along the street – motor car, tram, horse and cart, and bicycle. The building housing the Princes Cinema can be seen next to the second lamp post. The MacVitties Guest Restaurant behind the ornate ironwork was very popular with both its town and country customers for many years.

Life in the Town

Scotland was dominated in this period by the four great urban centres: Glasgow with a population of 784,455 in 1911, Edinburgh, population 320,318, Dundee, population 165,004, and Aberdeen, population 163,891, all depicted in these pages. However the smaller towns dominated their local area, the local market being an event which attracted the population for miles around. The trade of Haddington, the county town of East Lothian, with a population of 4140 in 1911, comprised mainly of agricultural produce and was one of the leading grain markets in Scotland. In 1912 the weekly market was held on a Friday: the sale of oats commencing at twelve noon, barley at twenty minutes past twelve o'clock, wheat at twenty minutes to one o'clock, and beans and peas at one o'clock. A fortnightly live stock auction was held on a Monday and a cattle fair was held in October.

The types of industry found in smaller towns was diverse, for example, Musselburgh, 6 miles east of Edinburgh in the county of Midlothian, had a population of 15,486 in 1911 and had major manufactories consisting of fishing net works, paper mills and a steel wire works and two large breweries, maltings and seed crushing works. Confectionery, potteryware, salt and skin mats were also made and boats built in the town.

The street scenes of the major conurbations, unlike other photographs of the period, do not just depict bustle and prosperity, the grime, poverty and underlying hardship are also there to be seen. An immediate difference to modern eyes is the lack of parked cars clogging up roads in the town and city streets.

Half the houses in Edwardian Scotland had only one or two rooms. The 1911 census recorded that 56 per cent of one-roomed houses (all rooms not just bed rooms) had more than two occupants, 47 per cent of two-roomed houses had more than two persons per room as did 24 per cent of three-roomed houses. Glasgow was the most overcrowded city in Great Britain with over half of its population living at a density of more than two people per room. In 1904 in Dundee a study of 6000 houses showed that 21 per cent of them had no sanitary accommodation for women and children, while 10 per cent of them had no such facilities for men. Almost a thousand houses had sanitary accommodation shared by thirteen to twenty-four persons, and 2000 had such accommodation shared by up to twelve people. The Canongate, High Street, Lawnmarket, and West Bow of Edinburgh, were all areas of overcrowding, dirt, near starvation and chronic poverty at the turn of the century.

Edinburgh Castle from the Esplanade, 24 February 1912.
On this sunny winter morning (Saturday? – there are too
many children about for a week day) two boys have made a
slide on the ice. The soldiers on the right appear to be
practising some sort of drill or are aiming to cull some of the
castle's visitors.

Princes Street, Edinburgh, 5 April 1912, under repair and not looking as though it was 'one of the finest streets in Europe'. However the Gothic Scott Monument, designed by a local architect, George Meikle Kemp, is a reminder of its grandeur. A policeman inspects the progress of the workmen. Note the special pick for lifting the setts from the road surface. The piles of horse dung would have been collected by a contractor and sold to farmers in the surrounding areas.

The dirt and dilapidation of the Canongate is all too visible in this photograph of Whitehorse Close, taken on 24 February 1912. The enamel 'five boys' advertisement for Fry's chocolate outside the confectioner's shop must have been a constant torment to children in an area where chocolate was a luxury. The push chair does not look very comfortable or safe and it must have been impossible for the clothes on the window pulleys to dry clean.

A cold, wet day in Whitehall Street, Dundee, February 1913. A fine sprinkling of snow can be seen on the roofs. The annual New Year sales are still on in this street in the heart of Dundee's shopping centre. Two heavily laden carts are pulled along the street by horses while a large trunk is carried by a man along the pavement, perhaps he is one of the many merchant seamen who frequented the city.

Tram No. 46 glides south along Reform Street, Dundee, February 1913. The electric lines powering the tram system can be seen criss-crossing the sky above the street, while the straight tram lines can be clearly seen in the road itself. The Albert Institute, a philosophical institute, housing a museum, reading-rooms and a picture gallery can be seen in the distance. Reform Street was designed by William Burn of Edinburgh and was one of the finest streets in Dundee in the style of its buildings and the splendour of its shops.

Street traders setting up their stalls outside the Royal Arch, Dundee on 1 February 1913. The arch, built of stone and ornately decorated, was situated on Mid Quay on the site of a wooden arch under which Queen Victoria and Prince Albert passed on their first visit to Dundee in 1844. Through the arch was to be found the Earl Grey Dock, covering five and a quarter acres, it is now filled in and a leisure centre and swimming pool occupies the site.

Union Street, Aberdeen, at Union Bridge, September 1914, looking east along one of the finest thoroughfares in the British Isles. The westward view along this street in the 'The Granite City' has been described as, 'suggesting to the imagination the tombs of Thebes, the Cyclopean walls, or the marble temples of ancient Greece'. The street has the air of a bustling city and there is no sign that the First World War, which Britain had joined a month earlier on 3 August 1914, has had any effect on this northern city.

The Mercat Cross in Castle Street, Aberdeen, 5 September 1914. The cross dates from 1686 when it replaced a medieval cross, which marked the centre of trade on market day. A group of children are buying something to eat from one of the stall holders while two boys look on with great interest. Some of the children are not wearing shoes. The shawl and apron of the woman walking with the toddler were typical of the clothing worn by working class women at this time.

May had been an exceptionally dry month in the east of Scotland in 1912 and the water level of the River Tyne at Haddington, East Lothian, was very low. The smell from the river was probably very high by the time this photograph was taken on the first of June and the removal of the debris in the river had begun. One cart is being loaded up and the tracks of its many previous trips can be clearly seen in the river bed. Local farmers had probably purchased the contents for spreading on their fields as manure. The boys in front of the weir are digging for bait for the fishing. The Nungate Bridge can be seen in the background.

Elgin an important agricultural town in north-east Scotland had a population of 8656 in 1911. One of the town's most cherished possessions are the ruins of Elgin Cathedral which are situated at its lower end. The cathedral dates from the twelfth century and is still known as the 'Lantern of the North'. It was being renovated by stonemasons when this photograph was taken on 22 September 1914. The wooden scaffolding does not look as though it would pass modern safety standards.

Musselburgh High Street, Midlothian, looking east, 30 March 1912. The two girls in the middle of the picture may be hoping that they are going to be treated by their adult companion to an ice cream from Di Rollo's. This shop had been established in Musselburgh by Italian, Domenico di Rollo in 1899 and has been well patronised ever since. The shop windows of Stirling Brothers, grocers and wine merchants are well stocked with goods and advertising signs. A very large load, perhaps a house removal, is being carted along the High Street but traffic is so light it is not the cause of any hold-up.

Inverness, the capital of the Highlands, had a population of 20,579 in 1911. The girl running across Muirtown Street on 23 September 1912 is perhaps going on an errand to the corner store. Behind the girl on the gable end are two fine examples of Edwardian advertising for 'Yorkshire Relish' and 'Whitbread Beer'. An ornate cast iron urinal and marble animal drinking trough stand in front of the wall. Both items, good examples of their type, are part of the lost street furniture of Scottish towns and cities.

Another piece of street furniture commonly seen in many Edwardian towns and villages was the water pump. Many houses within a town or whole villages were not connected to the main water system and water for all domestic requirements had to be collected from these cast iron pumps. In some rural parts of Scotland they were still in use until the early 1960s. Here a young girl is collecting water in a galvanised pail – note the stand for placing it on – outside Daniel Campbell's, a family grocers' shop in the High Street, Thurso, Caithness. The modestly clad cast iron drinking fountain was erected in 1898 in memory of Dr John Grant Smith, a former medical officer of the area.

High Street, Dingwall, the county town of Ross and Cromarty, 21 September 1912. Every Edwardian town contained all the retail shops and tradesmen that its inhabitants required in its main street. Dingwall was no exception and here we can see a hairdresser, draper, watch-maker, garage, toy bazaar, laundry, saddler (with a wonderful trade sign above the door), plumber and chemist. There was no need to visit a large city to obtain any item of purchase or service. However, the goods cascading on to the street would not be tolerated to-day.

Common Green, Strathaven, Lanarkshire on 29 June 1912. At the opposite end of Scotland from Dingwall we find a similar street scene in the market town of Strathaven. On this summer's day the shops on the sunny side of the street, Stewart Brothers, butchers and William Tennent, tailor and draper have put up their striped awnings to protect their window displays from damage by the sun. A group of boys are eagerly examining the window of the local printer and stationer, Nathaniel Bryson.

Miners from one of the coal seams in the vicinity of Prestonpans, East Lothian, worked by either the Summerlee Iron Co Ltd of Glasgow or Edinburgh Collieries Ltd, passing Mrs W F Jackson and a Miss Cameron on Prestonpans High Street on 6 September 1912. The miners's clothes, hands and faces are black as would be expected from their occupation and their lamps can be seen on the front of their helmets. They are just passing John Fowler & Co Ltd's brewery and malthouse which had been established in about 1720 in a former whisky distillery. In the distance a Sanderson's coal cart trundles along the street on the tramway.

One of the Miss Camerons window shopping in Coldstream High Street on 9 September 1911. The location of the fishmonger and chemist are clearly indicated by their trade signs. The local grocer with his long white apron has come out of his shop to speak to a passing friend or carter. The town was lit by gas and supplied with water under a scheme carried out by the Town Council. Bicycles appear to be a common form of transport in this Border town at the time.

Country Life

The vast majority of the land of Scotland in Edwardian times was rural, more so than today with urban developments eating into the countryside. However, by 1911 only one in twenty of the population was engaged in agriculture, forestry or horticulture, while just fifty years earlier one in eight of the population had been so employed. The overall population in rural areas was declining as people moved to the towns and emigrated, but life in the Scottish countryside was still vibrant. In many instances industrial centres were in a rural district and were not part of an urban development. The small market town of Prestonpans, East Lothian, which had a population of 1923 in 1911, consisted primarily of one long street running parallel with the Firth of Forth. Its manufactures comprised of earthenware, firebricks and other articles from fire-clay, common bricks, tiles, salt, beer, soap and coal.

Coldstream, Berwickshire, was typical of a vibrant Edwardian rural town or village where there was still a great local demand for tradesmen and shopkeepers like the blacksmith, joiner, fishmonger, chemist, saddler, baker, confectioner, butcher, watch-maker, ironmonger, painter, grocer, slater, stone mason, bootmaker, carter and drapers. Agricultural industries like grain milling, quarrying, forestry and leather tanning also thrived in the rural towns and villages.

The farming community in the Lowlands was dominated by the old landowners and tenant farmers while in the Highlands and Islands crofting had been put on a legal footing. Although the housing of the Lowland agricultural labourers looked superior to that of the Highland crofter the interior comforts, or lack of them, were very similar. Specialist farm labourers like 'bondagers' and 'hinds' were to be found in the fields of the Lowlands where labour intensive farming was to be the normal practice until the 1960s. Agricultural workers throughout the period were paid less than industrial workers and often received part of their wages in kind. A severe depression in British agriculture in the 1880s caused by large imports of wheat and meat, first from Eastern Europe and later from the United States, the Argentine, Australia and New Zealand, kept wages low and helped increase the movement from the country to town.

Farming techniques varied greatly over Scotland as a whole due to climate, terrain, land settlement and traditions. These differences occurred between the Highlands and Lowlands, between regions in the Lowlands, between districts and even between farms in the same area, as the variations in hay making demonstrate.

The town hall, Lauder, Berwickshire where the provost, baillies and councillors met to take decisions concerning the running of this royal burgh. The ornate gas lamp post in the centre of this photograph doubled as an animal drinking trough. Its supporting legs are in the shape of hooves. Despite having the status of a town the population of Lauder in 1911 was only 659.

The centre of Coldingham village, Berwickshire, 14 June 1913. Around the Cross have gathered the minister and two men whose conversation is being closely followed by a young boy. Perhaps they are waiting for the bootmaker to arrive with the keys for the recreation room so they can have a game of billiards. The cart standing outside the motorbus depot is definitely horse driven. Note the lion's head on the water pump.

Winter in the rural parts of Scotland was not as idyllic as this view might suggest. Houses had no central heating and roads were so bad that communities could be cut off for weeks at a time. Although the sun is shining on this January morning in 1913, the village of Daneshalt (Dunshelt), Fife, looks cold. The girl on the right of the photograph is not wearing a coat like her friends. Perhaps she is running a quick errand for her mother before going to school.

Grant's House, 16 May 1914. Grant's House was a small village in Coldingham parish in Berwickshire and a station on the North British railway line. It also had a post office and hotel. This is a stone quarry situated nearby which resulted in quantities of wood being available for local use as well as stone for further afield. The covered trucks have been filled with gravel and are awaiting removal. The machinery in the centre back of the photograph is for grading the size of the gravel.

A blacksmith at Ballencrieff Smithy, near Aberlady, East Lothian, inspecting stock in the yard, 19 April 1913. The smithy was run by David Tait and as well as shoeing horses and repairing farm machinery he was also an agent for Robin Hood Cycles. Many blacksmiths repaired bicycles and early motor cars, some in time becoming motor engineers. Note the puddles and state of the road. Most country roads were non-metallic at this time and were little more than dirt tracks.

The long, narrow strips of land, lazy beds, characteristic of much of crofting communities can be clearly seen in this photograph of Kyleakin, Skye, 1906. A two horse team is ploughing one of the central strips and the grazing cattle are free to wander across all the strips. The pier was built in the mid 1890s as a terminus quay for the Dingwall and Skye Railway, a steam ferry making the crossing between the mainland and Skye. The castle on the skyline is the thirteenth century keep, Castle Moil.

A long house, typical of the crofting community in the Hebrides, near Broadford, Skye, 1906. It is a single-storey house, built of large square boulders and roofed with reeds, tied and weighed down with stones. The second doorway leads into the byre for housing the animals of the croft. There was usually an internal connecting door to the byre. The walls were double thickness and there was a central fireplace with no chimney, the smoke being left to find its own way out, hence the smoke coming from the doorway and roof of the 'black house'.

A croft at Old Wick, near Wick, Caithness, 1 October 1912. Here the evolution of the long house can be seen. The living quarters are in the slated and chimney part of the building with the water butt at the front door. The byre is the building beyond this and the barn is the building to the back. The roofs of both the byre and barn are thatched. Hens are also in evidence and the large mound at the gable end of the building is the fuel stack of cut peats for heating and cooking.

Farm cottages at Saltcoats Farm, Gullane, East Lothian, May 1912. This group of six cottages is typical of their kind to be found in the Lothians. The pantiles on the roof would be orange/red in colour. Note the crow-stepped gable which gives a decorative extra lacking in the long houses. These cottages also have water barrels to collect rainwater from the roan. The farm labourers also had a small part of the communal garden at the back of the property in which to grow vegetables.

Bondagers, female farm workers at Kingston, near Dirleton, East Lothian hoeing weeds from the hedge rows, 21 April 1911. They are wearing the typical clothing of Edwardian Lothian female farm workers. They have stout boots on their feet; a skirt of drugget over a striped petticoat; gloves to protect their hands; a woollen shawl fastened tightly around their shoulders; and an 'ugly' on their heads as protection to the face and neck from the sun, wind and rain. The 'ugly' was a large bonnet made of gingham or coloured cotton cloth stretched over a light wicker frame forming a wide hood in front and a flap at the back.

These women are singling turnips at East Fortune, East Lothian, 24 July 1914. The growing of turnips for the winter feeding of cattle, in the days before silage, was labour intensive. The land would have been ploughed in November, cross ploughed in March or April and harrowed to break clods and clear weeds, twice ploughed between May and June and harrowed and cleaned again. The seed was sown in June and the drills were cleaned of weeds by horse-drawn equipment or by hand with hoes before the spacing or singling of the plants took place in July.

Hay making for winter fodder was a continuing process throughout the late spring and summer months. The hay was cut by a horse drawn mower and then left to dry, usually being turned by a horse drawn rake. The hay rake could also be used to gather the hay into piles prior to it being carted to the farm steading. Here a hay rake is at work in Gullane, East Lothian, 2 September 1911.

Haymaking at Muirfield Farm, Gullane, 27 June 1911. Two horse-drawn 'tummlin tams' are being used to gather the hay across the cut swathes. The gathered hay was forked into small ricks in the field for a further drying period. The line of ricks built in this field were probably lifted in one piece, with the aid of lifting gear, onto carts and led to the stackyard. Muirfield was farmed in 1911 by Thomas Fraser Ross.

Ploughing with a pair of horses near Oatfield Farm,
Dirleton, East Lothian, 12 April 1913. The 'hind' or
ploughman was a highly skilled labourer. He is wearing the
clothes of his job, stout boots, leggings to keep the earth off
his trousers, waistcoat, shirt and bonnet. Ploughing was
heavy work and on this windless day he has removed his
jacket. The ploughman was also responsible for the horses
that he worked and his day did not end until they were fed,
watered and groomed and began with the morning feeds
and mucking out.

On farms where the hay had been gathered into piles it was
then forked on to a cart. As the load grew higher so the
work involved in throwing the hay up on to the top grew
more difficult and strenuous. Eventually someone climbed
on to the top of the stack to ensure that the hay was secure.
Note the rope at the back of the cart for securing the load –
it has a stone tied to the end of it to weigh it down and thus
make it easier to throw over the high load. The labourers
are probably not enjoying the audience, Gullane,
2 September 1911.

Leading in the hay at West Fenton, Gullane, 25 July 1911. Once the rick of hay was transferred to a low cart and secured it was carted to the stackyard. The amount of loose hay lying on the grass verge indicates that this was not the first load of the day. The farmer at West Fenton was John B Handyside.

Stacking hay was a very tiring job. Here two stacks are being built at Muirfield Farm, Gullane, 6 July 1911, being fed by at least one cart each. Both stacks are now of a height that the labourers can only ascend and descend by ladder.

A platform has been erected on the right to act as a halfway-house for building the stack, which is already between fifteen and twenty feet in height. The workers on the top of the stack ensure that the hay is stacked correctly so that it will not fall over or overheat. Wooden staves are being used to give extra support to the stack.

At West Fenton Farm a different method is being used to build one long stack instead of several smaller ones. A pulley mechanism powered by the horse on the right lifts sections of the hay rick onto the stack where the labourers rake the hay into place. A single chain went around the section of the rick to be moved. This method was as labour intensive as the one employed at Muirfield Farm but it looks less stressful on the workers. The stack itself was built on a foundation of stone and once again staves are supporting the sides. Dated 25 July 1911.

The first combine-harvester, designed to cut, thresh and dress grain at the same time reached Scotland in 1932 in the form of a Clayton, a North American machine. It was used by Lord Balfour at Whittinghame Mains, East Lothian. Prior to, and after, that date and on many of the Islands and Highlands of Scotland today, the cutting and threshing of grain had to be carried out separately. Here a reaper is cutting wheat at Halbydown between Coldingham and Eyemouth, Berwickshire, 7 September 1912. The reaper bound the cut wheat into sheaves which were then stooked to dry before being led into the stackyard and stacked prior to being threshed.

A view of the harbour in Old Town, Stonehaven,
Kincardineshire, 15 March 1914. The town became a
fashionable summer resort during the Edwardian era, as it
was situated on a beautiful bay of the sea and had a railway
station on the Caledonian line. The harbour is a natural
basin, sheltered on the south-east and having a quay on the
north-east for loading and unloading ships with the
principal trade of the district, coal and lime. The herring
fishing fleet, all registered in Aberdeen, is at home.

Life by the Sea

Few parts of Scotland are more than forty miles from salt water and until the mid-twentieth century the country as a whole was linked, not separated, by water. The great firths of the Clyde, Tay and Forth assisted transport and contributed to the growth of towns and industry in the eighteenth and nineteenth centuries. Even with the coming of the railways, coastal towns still relied heavily on shipping as their main means of transport. Fishing was still a very important industry in Scotland during this period. In 1910 the total number of vessels engaged in the industry was nearly 10,000, valued at £5.75 million.

Herring fishing, undertaken with nets, was the most important branch of this industry with major centres at Eyemouth, Berwickshire; Stonehaven, Kincardineshire; Aberdeen; Wick, Caithness; Stornoway, Lewis; and Lochbroom, Ross and Cromarty. After herring came the deep sea 'white fishing' – cod, ling, haddock, sole, halibut and more – which at this period was pursued with baited lines but that was to be superseded by beam trawl nets. In 1907 the total weight of fish (excluding shell fish) landed in Scotland was over nine million tons. Large and small harbours supported fishing communities and ancillary trades such as fish processing, sail, net and rope making.

Dunbar, East Lothian, had a thriving crab and lobster fishing industry, most of its produce destined for the London market. Many of the small fishing ports became tourist attractions and sea resorts with the opening up of previously inaccessible villages such as Burnmouth, Berwickshire.

These inshore fishing boats are typical of those which plied the East coast of Scotland in the 1910s. Burnmouth, a small fishing village, in Ayton parish, Berwickshire, was one of only three safe anchorages between Berwick and Dunbar. The railway station on the North British line was situated on the cliff top, the village proper nestling at the bottom of steep cliffs. The fishermen would have been all too familiar with the Great Disaster on 14 October 1881, when a very violent storm hit the East of Scotland and four Burnmouth fishing boats were destroyed with the loss of twenty-four fishermen. 30 May 1914.

A thatched fisherman's cottage, Cromarty, Ross and Cromarty, 25 September 1912. The fisherman and women are preparing bait for the fishing lines which they are winding round the inside of a creel. Fishing nets, creels and baskets of varying sizes are piled up outside the cottage and dried fish on wooden spits are hanging on the outside walls. In 1913 about 193 fishing boats were engaged in Cromarty giving employment to 696 men and boys.

Women baiting fishing lines with mussels next to the harbour at North Berwick, East Lothian, 29 August 1912. North Berwick was a very popular summer resort by the end of the nineteenth century and its reputation increased with visits by King Edward during his reign. It was described as having a 'charming situation, noble views, and healthy climate'. Line fishing for white fish became unprofitable by the 1930s, seine-netting by steam trawlers having destroyed the breeding stock of fish.

Herring fishing nets drying in the wind at Elie, Fife, 1907. A pulley system allows the nets to be raised and lowered. The fishing boat is probably pulled up on the beach as its long oars can be seen on the grass bank. Elie had a fine reputation as a resort for summer sea-bathing.

Cat's Row, Dunbar, East Lothian, c.1907. This section of Dunbar housed the fisher folk who can be seen wearing their fishermen's hats, jerseys and long waterproof boots turned down at the knee. On this summer's day the washing hangs out to dry wherever there is room. The Milkmaid Brand Milk, illustrated with a milkmaid, and the yellow and blue Sunlight Soap enamel advertising signs were a common sight on walls in towns and villages.

Mr and Mrs W F Jackson in the garden at 'Glenlyon', Gullane dressed to attend a royal garden party at Holyrood Palace, Edinburgh, 20 July 1911. Mr Jackson is in full morning dress with gloves gold watch chain and an umbrella and Mrs Jackson has a high veiled and flowered hat, feather boa and matching parasol. Neither of them looks enthusiastic about the prospects for the day.

Mr and Mrs John Jackson, Junior, W F Jackson's brother and sister-in-law, in their best clothes, 22 July 1911. Mr Jackson is wearing a trilby hat and tweed suit with frock coat. Mrs Jackson has an appliqué tunic over her blouse and skirt. Note her long lace cuffs and the very fine feathers in her hat.

Fashion

At the beginning of the period, tailor-made costumes first appeared for women, the jackets had a masculine appearance but the skirts still reached the ground, and some day dresses still had trains. Dresses and skirts fitted tightly over the hips and were worn over high, stiffened corsets which pushed the body out at the back and up at the front, so that the overall effect was of an S-shape. Hats were worn on all formal occasions and were usually very large and heavily trimmed with feathers, flowers and ribbons. By the middle of the period curves gave way to a simpler shape but the dresses were still trimmed with lace, braid and buttons with parasols as an accompaniment. Long tunics were also worn over dresses during the day. The fashionable style then became one of a more drooping appearance as waists disappeared, a slimmer silhouette emphasised by perpendicular lines and narrow skirts. There was, of course, still a corset underneath. The growing trend, however, was to simpler less restrictive clothes with the coming of the motor car and increasing participation in sports.

Men's clothes were less uncomfortable than women's presumably owing to their earlier escape into sport where less restrictive clothes were required. Long frock-coats and tall silk hats were still worn on Sundays and formal occasions. The lounge suit had a long jacket, high-buttoned waistcoat and narrow trousers. The bowler hat had taken the place of the top hat for everyday apparel along with the shorter coat with the topper still worn on formal occasions. The trilby came into prominence after 1906.

Jenny Cameron in a cotton lace blouse and cotton printed skirt in the garden of 'Faussethill', 8 August 1914. Note her jewellery and the detail of the lace work.

Miss Janet Cameron at 'Glynlyon', 22 July 1911. She has put on the same tunic, which Mrs John Jackson was wearing in another photograph, over her light coloured silk blouse and cotton skirt. The detail can now be clearly seen. She is wearing a number of jewellery items: a ring, two bracelets, a brooch, pearls, pendant necklace and brooch. The buckle on her skirt belt is also exquisitely decorated with flowers.

Mrs L Peat has unwrapped her lace from its protective cloth and is painstakingly producing exquisite lace which she is also wearing on the cuffs and front of her blouse. Is the photograph in the pendant around her neck of her husband or father? 'Faussethill', 11 July 1912.

Mrs Robert Dickie a strong-willed old lady sitting in the garden of 'Faussethill', Gullane, 28 June 1913. Like most elderly widowed females, she is all in black except for the white lacing on her mop cap. Note her black lace mitts and braided cuffs and dress front.

At the other end of the age scale is Miss Daisy Jackson, the daughter of Mr and Mrs John Jackson, Junior, in the gardens behind Carlton Terrace, Edinburgh, 24 March 1913. She is swamped by a corduroy coat with an enormous collar tied with a large bow. Her hat would not look out of place on any female adult. Thick socks and woolly mitts keep out the cold.

Between the two age groups are the schoolgirl cousins,
Mary and Nellie Jackson and Nan and Peggy Snodgrass, at
'Faussethill', 27 July 1914. They are all wearing black
stockings and soft shoes and have their hair in bows but
that is where similarities in their apparel end. Mary is
wearing a summer frock, Nellie her sailor's top, Nan is
wearing a wide collared blouse and skirt, and Peggy a gym-
tunic.

Men had their fashions too. W F Jackson is in his smoking jacket at 'Glenlyon', 17 June 1911. Note the corduroy cuffs and collar and the decorative braiding. The upright collar must have been uncomfortable to wear.

Mr John Lattimer, Mrs W F. Jackson's brother, at 'Glenlyon', 2 September 1911. His matching waistcoat and trousers are covered by a long tweed jacket. The round celluloid collar was detachable for cleaning purposes.

Some exercise was taken at a leisurely pace illustrated by
this group out walking on the road from Dirleton to
Gullane, at Archerfield, East Lothian, 1 August 1911. They
are Mr and Mrs Duncan Cameron, Mrs W F Jackson's
sister and brother-in-law, from Glasgow, with their
daughter, Jenny and Mrs W F Jackson and Miss Edna
Carse. Mrs Jackson is wearing a coat in case of rain and
Miss Cameron has brought her umbrella but what has
happened to Edna's socks?

Leisure hours

The Church

The Christian church in Scotland during this period retained a greater hold over the population than in England and hundreds of thousands of middle and working class Scots regularly worshipped on the Sabbath, often attending up to three church services. There was a wide choice to make in the Edwardian period between the Church of Scotland (with communicants numbering 15 per cent of the population in 1902), the Free Church, the United Free Church (10 per cent), the Baptists, the Methodists, the Congregationalists, Scottish Episcopalian, Roman Catholic (10 per cent) and Methodists. The minister, in town and country, was an important and respected figure. Attendance at church gave respectability to the lower middle classes and the skilled working classes but the controversies which raged during the period between the sects appears to the modern eye to have been a total waste of the efforts of devout Christians.

The United Free Church to which W F Jackson belonged during this period was formed in 1900 on the amalgamation of the Free Church of Scotland and the United Presbyterian Church. The Free Church of Scotland had been formed in 1843 in the wake of the Disruption when almost 500 ministers had left the established Church of Scotland over the appointment of ministers. The new church raised over a million pounds within a few years and built over 650 churches. The United Presbyterian Church had been formed by an earlier defection from the Church of Scotland. The new United Free Church consisted of over 1100 Free Church congregations and over 600 United Presbyterian congregations. Nearly thirty Free Church ministers, most of them from the Highlands and Islands refused to accept the Union and the dispute over the rightful owners of the church buildings and funds of the former Free Church was not formally settled until 1905. Discussions for a merger between the Church of Scotland and the United Free Church began in 1909 and a plan for Union had been agreed by 1912 but it was not completed before the outbreak of the Great War and was only finally consummated in 1929.

However, the thousands of children who attended the Sabbath Schools of all the churches made life-long friends there and enjoyed the singing, stories and, of course, the annual picnic. The squabbling did not seem to touch them. It is indicative of the multitude of children attending the Sabbath School at Guthrie Memorial that the number of teachers was so great that they could organise a separate annual picnic just for themselves.

Sport and Recreation

Cricket, cross-country running, amateur and professional cycling races, croquet, lawn tennis, golf, ping pong (table tennis), hockey, association football, rugby football, skiing, and Swedish drill were all popular sports during the Edwardian period. Quoits, bowling and curling were popular as village sports and croquet, lawn tennis, golf, table tennis, skiing and Swedish drill were being actively pursued by women. Golf, in particular, at this time was growing enormously as a national and international sport and leisure industry.

Both Gullane and North Berwick in East Lothian capitalized on their rail and golf links. There was a special Saturday train service for golfers bound for Gullane and North Berwick Town Council achieved a concessional fare on the railway, between the town and Edinburgh, for the members of North Berwick Corporation Golf Clubs. By the 1900s North Berwick was being publicised as the 'Biarritz of the North' and it was the fashionable society's choice as a golfing and holiday resort.

Holidays

The Jackson family was well off and could afford to take a house for the summer, at the fashionable Scottish sea-side resort – Dunbar in 1904 and Gullane from 1908 to 1912. Here W F Jackson would leave his wife and niece during the week, coming down at weekends and for his annual leave. The Jacksons also visited other fashionable resorts on the English south coast, such as Margate, Broadstairs, Ramsgate, Tunbridge Wells, Brighton, Eastbourne, Worthing, and Bournemouth, as well as the Continent, travelling extensively in Germany (in 1902 and 1908), Ireland (1904), France (1905), the Channel Islands (1907), and Denmark, Sweden and Norway (1913). In the winter of 1909–10 the Jacksons and Camerons sailed to and travelled around Egypt on a Cook's Tour. They also travelled throughout Scotland, usually via the North British line on which W F Jackson, as general manager had a free pass. *The Highland Witness* of 1904 states that Mr and Mrs Jackson's favourite holiday destination was Norway, owing to the country's grand scenery and its hardy inhabitants.

While on domestic or foreign trips, the Edwardians delighted in sending postcards to friends and collecting them as souvenirs of their visits. Every newsagent, stationer and general store sold them. It has been estimated that during this period about ten million postcards were being sold every week in Britain.

At the Seaside

The seaside with its healthy fresh air became a favourite destination for a holiday or a day's outing. Shorter working hours and the Saturday half-day holiday led to many more people escaping to the sea-side for a short break from the daily routine. The revolution in transport with the coming of the train, the automobile and the motor bus enabled more people to travel to the seaside for paddling, picnics, or the pierrots. Sea bathing became a very healthy and popular pas-time and bathing costumes which had been very cumbersome items of apparel – navy blue serge with high necks, long sleeves, and skirts over baggy, calf-length legs, befrilled and trimmed with white braid – gave way to the one-piece stockinette costume which was much more prac-tical but still not very becoming.

The Ladies' (unmarried) Race ready to start at the Guthrie Memorial United Free Church Sabbath School teachers' picnic at Aberlady, East Lothian, 8 July 1911. Skirts are hitched up for the off but one lady at least is going to attempt the race without removing her gloves, jacket or large, delicately balanced hat. The minister of Guthrie Memorial, A St Clair Sutherland is standing behind the start line.

And they are off and running and not a hat in sight among the front runners. From the smiles on the teachers's faces everyone was enjoying themselves.

The married teachers at Guthrie Memorial were not left out of the fun but they were not allowed to run. Their race was to be taken at walking pace only. Mrs W F Jackson doing battle at Aberlady during the Married Ladies' Walking Race, 8 July 1911.

Picnic time at the Sunday School trip of St Mary's United
Free Church, Edinburgh, to Niddrie, on the outskirts of
Edinburgh, 6 June 1914. The children are so intent on not
missing out on the food and drink that few of them are
aware of the camera.

Swedish drill, working out with Indian clubs, was an
energetic form of exercise. Miss Jeanie Cameron and Miss
Netta Forshaw, clad in gym-slips, working their way
through an exhausting routine with their clubs,
'Faussethill', 11 April 1914.

Croquet was a very popular summer game but Miss Lizzie Reid appears in this photograph rather overdressed to play. Her skirt is restrictive but her veiled and flower covered hat looks secure. 'Shalimar', Strathaven, Lanarkshire, 5 July 1913.

Mrs W F Jackson was a very competitive woman. Here she is playing bowls against her brother-in-law, Robert Jackson, in the garden of his house, 'Arduli', at Inveresk, Midlothian, 10 August 1910. The carpet on the lawn is to give extra grip when bowling. Note the short, even cut to the grass which has been mown with a machine.

Golf became a very popular game during the Edwardian era and it was played by both men and women. Mrs R M Readdie, Mrs W F Jackson's sister, putting on Archerfield Golf Links, Gullane, East Lothian, 15 July 1915. Sometimes it was necessary to tie a scarf around the hat to keep it in place when teeing off.

One of the foursome was Mr John Reid who is about to putt the ball. Gullane by this time had become the leading golfing resort south of St Andrews. There were two golf club makers in the village, Edwin Sinclair and Alexander Aitken who also made golf balls.

Mr and Mrs W F Jackson and Miss Nellie Jackson sitting on
deck chairs on the P & O steam ship *Persia* in the
Mediterranean *en route* to Egypt in the winter of 1909–1910.
Miss Janet Cameron accompanied the Jacksons on this
Thomas Cook trip to the Middle East. Mrs Jackson is
knitting while Mr Jackson is reading *The Scrap Book*, an
Edwardian periodical.

Miss Nellie Jackson and Mr and Mrs W F Jackson on
donkeys near Medinet Haboa, Thebes, Egypt. The ladies
are riding side saddle and the barefooted natives look as
though they are experienced in front of a camera. Mr
Jackson is expressionless behind his dark glasses.

One of the Sphinxes at Pompey's Pillar, Alexandria, Egypt.
Mr Jackson and his sister, Nellie, looked hot and tired
leaning against the plinth, owing to overdressing perhaps?
Mr Jackson gave two lectures entitled 'Bible Sites and
Scenes' and 'Some of the Occupations Mentioned in the
Bible' in Dumbarton in December 1918 illustrated by slides
of similar views of Egypt.

Having tea on the verandah of the Hotel in Mallaig, Inverness-shire, c.1906. The weather here is much colder as the thick jacket and fur wrap suggest. Mrs Jackson has purchased postcards to send to friends for their collections and Mr Jackson's hatted shadow can be clearly seen taking the photograph.

Neidpath Castle, near Peebles, Peeblesshire, 7 February 1914. A striking view of the castle from the south bank of the River Tweed. The castle at this time was falling into disrepair as can be seen on the right hand side where part of the tower has collapsed. The overall feeling conveyed by the photograph, however, is one of romance.

John O'Groats, Caithness, as the most northerly inhabited
point on the British mainland, has been a tourist attraction
since the mid-nineteenth century. The post office run by
George Mason, who was also licensed to sell tobacco, is
displaying postcards and other souvenirs in its windows.
Whose tea was the best in the world? Dated 30 September
1912.

Miss Maclean's circulating library and fancy repository,
Strathpeffer, Ross and Cromarty, 24 September 1912.
Strathpeffer was a fashionable health resort, popular for
the whole four month summer season and renowned for its
medicinal wells. Its waters were the most powerful in
Scotland and cures were commonly taken by drinking the
waters although sulphur, brine and peat baths were also
widely used. Miss Maclean's shop is full of souvenirs and
china and pottery items while outside there are walking
sticks, a china display case, cane baskets and postcards,
produced by Tuck's.

Miss M J Cameron, Miss E McGhie, Mrs W F Jackson and
Miss J I Cameron wading in the sea at Gullane, East
Lothian, 9 August 1912. The women have removed their
stockings but not their hats to go paddling.
Note Jenny Cameron's wrist watch.

Mr W F Jackson has removed his hat, jacket and rolled up his trouser legs to go wading at Gullane, 5 August 1911. His expression is inscrutable.

Mary and Nellie Jackson have removed all their outer clothes and are paddling in the sea in their underclothes, Gullane, 22 July 1911. Mary is in her combinations and Nellie is wearing a modesty bodice and frilly bloomers. Mary is warning her father that she does not want him to get any closer.

Mary Jackson in her swimming costume, Gullane, 6 June 1911. Now she can get completely wet if she wants without ruining her clothing. Note the bathing cap to keep her long hair dry.

Mr W F Jackson has decided to take the plunge and is bathing in the sea at Gullane in June! For the photograph he is in shallow water lying on the sand. This is one of the most expressive photographs of William in the collection. 26 June 1912.

The major problem encountered at the seaside is removing sand from the toes when it is time to leave. Here Miss Janet Cameron and Mrs W F Jackson are sitting on the rocks at Gullane, drying their feet and putting on their stockings and shoes. 12 July 1912.

One of the delights of being at the seaside at North Berwick during the summer season was the entertainment. The Pierrots, dressed in their familiar black and white costumes, are performing on the open stage at the esplanade near the harbour, 4 July 1911. With an afternoon and evening performance the Pierrots were led at this time by Fred Erick.

The party having a picnic on the beach at Gullane, 9
August 1912, consist of Jenny Cameron, Mrs W F Jackson,
Mrs D McGhie, Miss M McGhie, Marion Cameron, and
Miss E McGhie. The sandwiches are in an old MacVitties
biscuit tin and the thermos flasks have been used to make a
hot drink, perhaps cocoa, although some sort of soft drink
is available in bottles.

Mrs John Jackson, Senior, sitting in a carriage at Tantallon, near North Berwick, 30 June 1911. Perhaps Mrs Jackson is visiting friends or the younger family members may be exploring the castle and have left their grandmother in the shade to rest. The carriage may have been hired for the day or lent by friends. The coachman is very smartly dressed.

Getting About

The nineteenth century revolution in transport had an enormous impact upon the lives of the Scottish people. The age of the railways and the coming of the motor car, motor bus and motor lorry did not yet detract from the age of the horse as the main means of transport by horse drawn carriage, cart and tram. Many people could not afford to go any other way but on foot and this was the case in the towns as well as the countryside. However, the coming of the railways brought far-reaching social change. The population were able to move around and enjoy many more pleasure pursuits. To many seaside resorts the coming of the railway led to a greatly increased number of visitors.

By 1901 cars had taken their modern shape, with the engine in front of the driver but they were high and roofless. Driving on non-tarmac roads was extremely dusty and drivers and passengers alike wore driving coats, which were long and enveloping. Women often wore motoring veils to hold down their hats. By 1904 the speed limit stood at 20 miles per hour and the compulsory registration of motor cars introduced on the first of January that year indicate that there were some 8500 motor cars in the whole of Great Britain. The bicycle too produced a minor social revolution. It brought the countryside within the reach of the urban worker and allowed the luxury of living further from work and consequently a measure of choice in employment. It also led to a change in women's clothing as long skirts and cycling were positively dangerous.

The High Street, North Berwick, East Lothian, 14 July 1911. The notice on the wall points the way to the premises of George Bell, coach proprietor of Law Road, where landaus, wagonettes, brakes and pony traps were for hire. The women may be going for a game of bowls or for a walk up the Law. Note the workman returning home with a milk pitcher and a bunch of flowers for the woman at home.

Mr and Mrs W F Jackson, Mr and Mrs R M Readdie and
the Misses Croall out for a drive in a trap near Dunbar,
East Lothian, in the summer of 1905 or 1906. Miss Mary
Readdie (Massie) is asleep in her mother's arms. The trap is
being pulled by two ponies and the driver is wearing the
familiar top hat.

The North British Railway Station at Peebles, Peeblesshire,
was opened on 4 July 1855. When the train deposited its
passengers at the station there were horse-drawn vehicles
on hand to deliver the travellers to their final destination.
A horse and cart and hansom cab wait patiently at the
entrance of the station in Northgate, 7 February 1914.

North British Railway locomotive No. 302 with coal tender
and three coaches at Gullane Railway Station, 19 August
1914. Gullane won fourth prize in the best-kept station
competition in 1912. The flower beds are tidy and colourful
and there is no litter to be seen on the platform. The name
of the station appears in white lettering on the back of the
bench.

Gullane was described in the North British Railway *Official Tourist Guide* for 1915 as 'a pretty village possessing the unique advantage of having several magnificent beaches and a sandy beach stretching for miles'. Two golfers are about to board the first class compartment, while John Seth, the station master, stands by the door. The John Menzies' bookstall carried a large stock of books, newspapers and magazines. 19 August 1914.

The railway station at Bo'ness, Linlithgowshire, was a long
single-storied building with the ticket office in the middle,
under the cornice. The walls of the station are covered with
advertisements for soap and furniture and railway
timetables and notices about special trains to London. The
hand barrow may be carting items to or from the station.
Note the washing drying on the fence. 30 April 1913.

St Enoch Station, on the Glasgow District Subway, 22 February 1913. The Jacobean-style station was built in the 1870s and in 1913 proclaimed from its roof-top that it could offer a subway for Hillhead, Markinch, Ibrox and Govan every three minutes. The times of the trains and the subway route are posted on notices around the station.

Kirkcaldy Corporation locomotive and North British Railway trucks at the harbour, Kirkcaldy, Fife, January 1913. The new harbour, extending to four and a half acres, was opened in 1909. The quayage extended over 1000 yards and a branch of the main line railway traversed its entire length. Kirkcaldy was a port and manufacturing town of repute in the early decades of this century.

The first Scottish motor car was built in 1895 and soon
proved popular. W F Jackson tried out the new invention
and often hired a car to drive around East Lothian during
the summer holidays. It was said that he forbade anyone to
drive at speeds over 15 miles per hour. Here he is driving his
wife and Jenny Cameron sometime before April 1906. The
passengers and driver have taken precautions against the
coldness of the wind and are wearing thick coats.

A small group of girls have gathered outside the grocers to watch another new-fangled vehicle go through its paces in the Square, Portsoy, Banffshire, 7 September 1914. The passenger in the side-car is leaning over to the left to keep the motor-cycle balanced.

The swings in the George Allan Park, Strathaven, Lanarkshire, 29 June 1912. A mother and father are keeping a watchful eye on their children. The notice on the top of the swings states that these are 'for BOYS ONLY Under 15 Years – Turns Not To Exceed 5 Minutes Each'. At least one regulation is being broken because two girls can be seen having a turn.

Family Life and Children at Play

The popular image of family life in the Edwardian period is still one of Victorian strictness. Families were still very large in comparison to those of the late twentieth century and the population of Scotland in the Edwardian period was much younger than it is today. Children were always seen if they were not to be heard. The formal clothes that children are wearing, especially on the beach, seem over-dressed to our eyes with the girls in bonnets, pinafores, petticoats, long stockings, bows, ribbons, heavy shoes, and the boys in suits, waistcoats, jackets, caps and heavy boots. Although the children are dressed as young adults they are, at least in these photographs, smiling and enjoying themselves. There is a hint that the stern 'paterfamilias' of the Victorian era has given way to some extent to the 'family man'.

A maypole in the George Allan Park, 29 June 1912. The children are watching and waiting for a turn to swing round the pole. Girls were probably officially banned from this activity as well.

Miss Massie Readdie acting as caddie on Archerfield Golf links, Gullane, East Lothian, 15 July 1911. Her buttoned shoes would be very fashionable today but the thin cotton dress looks as though it could be easily torn.

A little gypsy from an itinerant gypsy family at Cat's Back, Strathpeffer, 24 September 1912. Gypsies travelled around Scotland undertaking seasonal farm work. The girl is barefoot and it looks as though neither she nor her clothes have been cleaned in weeks. The purpose of the animal skins is a mystery.

Children will be children wherever there is water to be found, Coldstream, Berwickshire, 1905 or 1906. The boys wear bonnets like their fathers and some of their clothes have certainly seen several owners. The girls on the bank have decided not to get wet.

Three girls and a teddy bear at Swanston, near Edinburgh, 28 Februrary 1914. They are probably the children of a farm labourer on Swanston Farm. Swanston Cottage was the summer residence of Robert Louis Stevenson, the famous Edinburgh author, from 1867 to 1880 and this made the village a popular tourist attraction.

Sailor suits were popular for boys and girls at this time. Master Robert and Peter Lennox Snodgrass are trying to look innocent but one suspects that they are itching to pull Edna Carse's pigtails. 'Glenlyon', Gullane, 5 August 1911.

An official family photograph of Mr and Mrs John Jackson, Junior, and their daughters, Mary and Nellie, at 'Glenlyon', Gullane, East Lothian, 22 July 1911. It extols the virtues of family life and the good manners and behaviour of the children.

The John Jackson, Junior, family at play, 'Glenlyon',
Gullane, 22 July 1911. The unofficial photograph showing
that the Jacksons were fun-loving and not afraid to tickle
Daddy while he is held on the ground.

Bibliography and Sources

Donnachie, Ian and Macleod, Innes, *Victorian and Edwardian Scottish Lowlands from Historic Photographs*, BT Batsford, London (1979).

Dundee Social Union, *Report on Housing and Industrial Conditions in Dundee*, John Leng & Co Ltd, Dundee (1905).

Ferrier, Rev Walter M, *The North Berwick Story*, Royal Burgh of North Berwick Community Council, North Berwick (1980).

Hill, C W, *Edwardian Scotland*, Rowman and Littlefield, Totowa, New Jersey (1976).

Minto, C S, *Victorian and Edwardian Scotland From Old Photographs*, BT Batsford, London (1970).

North British Railway, *The Beauties of Scotland, Official Tourist Guide*, Edinburgh (1915).

Oliver, George, *Photographs and Local History*, BT Batsford, London (1989).

Oliver, George, 'The Lind Collection (1) and (2)', *The Scots Magazine*, New Series, vol. 112, No. 4 (January and February 1980) pp. 406–417 and 500–506.

Thomas, John, *The North British Railway, Vol 1 and 2*, David and Charles, Newton Abbot (1969 and 1975).

Edwardian East Lothian, The Journeys of W F Jackson, East Lothian District Library and Gullane Local History Society (1989).

120 Photographic Gems of Scottish Scenery, John Leng & Co Ltd (n.d. c.1900).

'Men You Know – No. 1473', *The Bailie*, Vol. LVII, No. 1473 (9 January 1901).

Obituary of 'Mr W F Jackson', *Glasgow Herald* (2 December 1931).

Obituary of 'The late W F Jackson', *Scotsman* (2 December 1931).

'Prominent Laymen of our Church', No. III, *The Highland Witness*, No. 11 (1904).